Remembering
Paris

Editorial Direction
Ghislaine Bavoillot
Editorial Management
Nathalie Bailleux
Design
Jocelyn Kargère
Typesetting
Dominique Grosmangin
Production
Murielle Vaux
Photoengraving
Colorscan, France

Published simultaneously
in French under the title
Je me souviens de Paris.
Copyright © 1998 Flammarion,
Paris.

For the English translation:
Copyright © 1998 Flammarion.
All rights reserved. No part
of this publication may be
reproduced in any form
or by any means, written,
electronic, information
retrieval system, or photocopy
without written permission
from Flammarion.

Translated from the French
by David Radzinowicz Howell

Edited by Sheila O'Leary

Flammarion
26 rue Racine
75006 Paris

ISBN: 2-08013-659-3
Numéro d'édition: FA365908
Dépôt légal: September 1998
Printed and bound by
G. Canale & Co. SpA
Printed in Italy
Library of Congress
Catalog Card Number: 98-073615

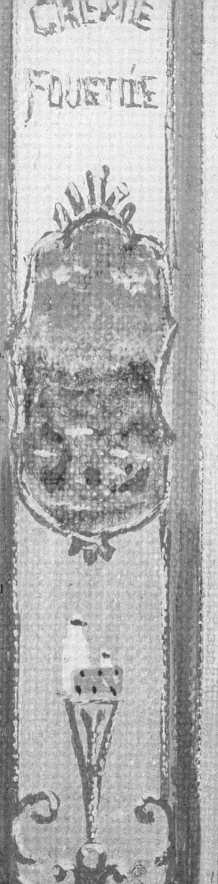

For my parents
Denis Tillinac

For Lala
André

Denis Tillinac

André Renoux

Remembering
Paris

Flammarion
Paris - New York

To go from Ile de la Cité to Ile Saint-Louis across the Pont de l'Archevêché is to travel from the fervor of the Middle Ages into the icy perfection of the Classical era.

Memories, Memories

For a long time, I loathed this city that cast such a shadow over my childhood, confining it to the fifth floor of an apartment building without an elevator on Avenue Daumesnil. It is a neighborhood that cannot be said to wear its poetry on its sleeve. Its only concession to my dreams of escape was the area around the little station known as Reuilly: one can always imagine that a suburban train might switch to the wrong rails and speed off towards the countryside. At the end of the avenue, the Porte Dorée opened a window on the exotic by dint of the Musée des Colonies and the zoological gardens, all that is left of the Colonial Exposition of 1931.

I went to school at the Oratorians of Saint-Michel behind the Picpus cemetery where itinerant Americans would endeavor to steel their patriotism at the tomb of La Fayette. As a result of my misbehavior, the school and I agreed to part company and I was enrolled with other Oratorians at the École Massillon situated in a fine old early eighteenth-century mansion, which had been ruined by anachronistic baroque extensions added during the nineteenth century. It is to be found on the edges of the Marais quarter, opposite the Bibliothèque de l'Arsenal. Schoolboys are not susceptible to architectural style: all their poetry is encompassed by marbles and footballs. The square at the end of the Ile Saint-Louis served as our pitch. Sometimes the ball would fall into the Seine. We would hail the rivermen as their barges slid slowly under the arches and went off to recover the longed-for object on the Quai d'Anjou towpath. A staircase still allows one to reach it, but barges are less frequent.

One has to have reached the age of those that love Peynet to be able to savor fully the charm of that triangle set with bushes over which the statue of the animal sculptor Barye reigns. Further upstream, the great metal arch of the Pont d'Austerlitz, the glass windows of the Grande Bibliothèque and the concrete of the new Bercy complex—a world yet unfinished whose straight-edge lines remind one of the paintings of Bernard Buffet. I like it better downstream: the dark spire of Notre-Dame rising between its twin towers, the Pont de la Tournelle with its whitish statue of Sainte Geneviève, the belltower of Saint-Gervais, the giraffe-like neck of

I have always considered the towpath by Quai d'Anjou on the Ile-Saint-Louis (above) as the perfect place for a romantic walk. Many is the stroll I took there, but alone, unfortunately, while the steeple of Saint-Gervais loomed above as though to mock me from the other riverbank.

The apex of Quai de Bourbon is like the prow of a ship which has cast off the moorings we have made for it, and loosed itself from the confines of this ordinary world to become a shadowy temple of the most secret and sensual delights (opposite).

the Eiffel Tower, the narrow mouth of the Rue Saint-Louis-en-l'Ile.

I often return to wander on the Pont Sully. At night, shady individuals lurk at the back of the square. Protected from prying eyes by an ivy-clad wall, the Hôtel Lambert seems to float towards some unreal realm. By chance, I had occasion to dine there once with the lady of the domain. It was like a flashback—I could see my childhood through the tower window. It was not very far away.

One cannot pass Quai des Orfèvres on the Ile de la Cité without imagining oneself under arrest in the office of Simenon's famous detective Maigret (opposite). But guilty of what crime? Of stealing the poetry of Paris.

Long ago, there were houses, small shops, street artists, alchemists, fortune-tellers, pickpockets, and good-time girls on the Pont Neuf (above).

11

This same childhood winks at me whenever I go to dine at the Orangerie walking down the Rue Saint-Louis-en-l'Ile where the wooden frontages have been preserved and painted: Berthillon in light-brown, Castafiore in royal blue and the Ilot Vaches, red. Gazing at the wrought-iron openwork belltower of the church of Saint-Louis, I recall how I heaved open the carriage door to a neighboring apartment building and climbed from floor to floor to take private lessons with my Latin professor, the author Jean Markale. At the time he sported a less Celtic-sounding name and the rich were not yet living on that enchanted island. One would bump into tramps pushing their rags along in prams. At dusk, the street had all the look of a haunt for footpads and one almost expected villains armed to the teeth to rush out of Rue

Poulletier. If ever there were any, they have long since vanished. When the restaurants close up, couples can be seen window-shopping and making their way to the end of the island, or else on the Quai Bourbon where they embrace, their eyes turned to the belltower of Saint-Gervais behind an uneven line of roofs—the Hôtel de Ville, the Théâtre du Châtelet, the Saint-Jacques tower, while glass-roofed tourist barges pass beneath the Pont d'Arcole. Later, they might saunter on the river's edge reading the plaques mounted on the Grand Siècle facades. Here lived Princess Bibesco, Hector Daumier, Philippe de Champaigne, "painter and manservant to the Queen Mother." Such a job description confirms me in my allergy to state-subsidized art: if the Prince pays, one has to become his valet. Better to remain free, I say to myself,

A facetious play on words transforms the old Ile-aux-Vaches ("island of cows", once part of the present Ile Saint-Louis) into an island of restaurants (above). If you think you see one of those horned creatures it is because you've drunk too much.

When night falls the clocks turn back on Quai de Bourbon, and you too can become another Baudelaire lost in an artificial paradise (opposite).

walking round the island, late at night, with the heady sensation of floating in some suspended fairyland. While the freshly gilded gutters and balconies of the Hôtel Lauzun force me to admire them, I am more touched by the diminutive Hôtel Marigny with its improbable balcony perched above the gateway. I dream of some duchess held prisoner by her languor—or else in the frenzy of some unspeakable passion....

To reach Massillon, one has to take the Métro to Bastille—we used to say "la Bastoche." This segment of the canal framed by the Boulevard Bourdon endowed the place with mystery and

Whenever the eye strays skyward, one spies washed-out gray roofs whose lack of symmetry nonetheless leads to a paradoxical harmony.

ambivalence. The quarter is at once famous and infamous. Fire-eaters, sword-swallowers, conmen take up their positions in front of the Métro entrance. I would linger there before admiring the harnessed steeds of the Garde Républicaine on the Boulevard Henri IV. One day, I caught sight of General de Gaulle in the flesh, inside a Citroën DS 19, sporting his kepi with its two stars.

The Bastille has been mutilated by the hideous new camembert-shaped Opera House. To recapture the carefree atmosphere of the Balajo's salad days one has to make one's way down Rue de la Roquette, or the Faubourg Saint-Antoine that has kept its original flavor beyond Avenue

Pont Neuf, which is actually more than one bridge since it straddles both branches of the Seine, was the largest in the world during the reign of Henri IV, who is duly commemorated by a statue.

Ledru-Rollin by Square Trousseau. There one can find down-at-heel bars where secretaries with luridly painted lips put up with the usual repartee.

The outskirts of Daumesnil have not been spared either. The destitute Gare de Reuilly dies a lingering death among a forest of blocks, like the crocodiles in the tank of that colonial museum whose name has since had to be changed—one more nail in the coffin of the adventure that was the Empire. This apart, the Porte Dorée has hardly altered. It served as an "open sesame": in the summer vacation, the paternal *Frégate* would turn into the outer boulevards before joining the trunk roads. I still have a liking for the city's thresholds, dotted with brick buildings and brasseries where early juke-boxes used to play Elvis's first 45s. Adults preferred Edith Piaf whose heart-rending tones can still bring back to me the Paris of the accordionist that I knew in my tender years—the same Paris that the painter Renoux celebrates in his cards showing a Morris advertising column,

a Wallace fountain, a florist's cart, or a glazed plaque—all waiting at the crossroads of my memory.

For me, Renoux's wander down memory lane recaptures an imaginary city that I can recognize, with his laudable bias for carless streets, roofs without TV aerials, and deserted restaurants. Memory is better stirred when there are no human figures: their obsolescence only sullies the marriage between past and present, whereas, in the painter's own private time machine, it can be celebrated in harmony.

I wanted to lay eyes once more on the Picpus cemetery where—among other victims of political savagery—the spirit of the poet André Chenier has its abode. It is here too, in nameless trenches, that those guillotined during the Terror are buried. Behind a wall the pupils of Saint-Michel could be heard yelping. The years that separate us seemed short to me: I am like the shadow of an adult who is forever re-creating himself.

All those comfortable novels set in Paris play host to a now extinct species: the concierge, scourge of burglars and illicit lovers, always there with her bell and her police contacts.

My Life Begins

Once I was an adolescent, I left Paris. I returned with a *baccalauréat* I had obtained by the skin of my teeth and the idea of drifting into whatever took my fancy. At twenty, a city is the mirror image of our own impatience. One is blind to one's surroundings, obsessed with the search for ecstasy, love, and any other sort of extreme. One is oblivious to its accepted beauties, an inclination to anarchy drawing one to its fringe life. I preferred the dark, bucolic quality of the Père-Lachaise cemetery, the gaudy stalls of the Rue Belleville and Ménilmontant, the trench opened up by the twist of rails between Saint-Lazare and the Pont Cardinet. I adored the ambiguity of doorways, the sadness of railway stations, the stagnant waters and dark sluice gates of the Saint Martin canal, the plebeian fun of the Grands Boulevards between République and the Théâtre de Saint-Martin, the dreary despair of the Boulevard Sébastopol, the glimpses into the private life of others offered by the overhead section of the Métro between Étoile and Nation, in particular the stretch by Barbès.

You have Paris at your feet when you walk down the steps of Rue Utrillo, and the mere mention of that crazy painter is enough to give you the soul of an artist (above).

The artist Francisque Poulbot also richly deserves his street on the slopes of the hill (opposite) for immortalizing that most loveable of Parisian characters—the street urchin—along with Victor Hugo's character, Gavroche.

PATACHOU

Each to his own *Guermantes' Way*. Mine led me to lengthy wanderings beneath Pigalle's neon lights, punctuated by stops at the champagne-girl bars on Rue Fontaine whenever my financial state allowed. Twenty is also an age at which money is in short supply. Thanks be, there was always to be found, on the corners of the streets which rise towards the hillock between Anvers and Place Blanche, the sort of whores Blaise Cendrars would have met and from whom one might procure for the sum of sixty francs (new-style) an instant of relief without too much attendant risk. One had to count ten francs for the madam, in exchange for a piece of soap and a towel, and on occasion a word of encouragement. Apart from Pigalle, business was carried out behind the Porte Saint Denis, around the central market halls—prior to their suburban exile—and a street backing onto the Gare de Lyon whose name escapes me.

My childhood religiosity found its own place of worship: the old Parc des Princes with the banked bends of its racetrack where Marche's Racing would do battle with Raymond Kopa's team from Reims. One got there by leaping on the rear platform of bus number 62. I also went to see the French team play at the Colombes stadium by taking the commuter train from Saint-Lazare. It remained for me to pay hommage at one of the two temples standing on the ring road: Jean-Bouin and Charlety, both dating from the 1920s. Their decrepitude, the fervor of the initiates piled up in the stands gave the excuse for a flight *extra muros*, beyond the cares of the world, towards that

There is plenty of bad painting on the Place du Tertre (opposite) and a surplus of tourists at Patachou (above), but the magic of both places, coupled with a birds-eye view of the city, make up for such drawbacks.

A delightful jewel of Romantic architecture, the Théâtre de l'Atelier lies at the cusp of the Montmartre beloved of artists, scoundrels, and the well-off (following double page).

never-never land to which I had been summoned, in a very different manner, by the wild beasts of the zoo at Vincennes and the Gregorian chant of the Dominican services.

The rebirth of the Stade Français sometimes takes me back to the Jean-Bouin stadium which has remained much as it was, a haven of fellow-feeling in the shadow of a somewhat impersonal Parc des Princes. Colombes has been robbed of its grandstand and its status as a place of pilgrimage. A shining, metallic Charlety set forth its shoots not long ago, and now High Mass in honor of the oval or round ball is celebrated on the Saint Denis plain where the Kings of France are laid to rest. In my own private symbolism, the proximity of these two basilicas is not without significance.

The clock of life swings back and forth with each quest for love and with each writer one encounters. My map of Paris has acquired some startling relief thanks to my discovery of the novels of Georges Simenon. They rudely awakened me to the dying embers of a whole civilization and to the birth of that wretched character caught up in a morass of uncontrollable desires that we call modern man. Having lost everything that might serve to anchor him, he totters on the edge of desolation before plunging into the void. Was I too just a straw to be blown about on the winds of a desire I could never express? I had good reason to fear it was true.

Not many people are aware that the Moulin de la Galette was the scene of a heroic act during the time that the uhlans occupied Paris following the defeat at Sedan (above).

On the most secretive slope of the hill, on the Rue du Chevalier-de-la-Barre where the vines overlook the Saint-Denis plain, the already famous Stade de France can be glimpsed in the distance (opposite).

A stroll around the Place du Tertre at night, in the depths of winter and in the rain, is a must: one can sense the spirits of a host of artists, and the imagination is spoiled for choice.

When he was twenty, Simenon turned up beneath the vaulted roof of the Gare du Nord with the kind of appetites that remain *de rigueur* after a protracted war. He hailed from Liège. I too came from elsewhere and was no less hungry. A wife to whom he had been bound in the euphoria of the Armistice soon joined him. She was a painter. They settled in Montmartre, surprisingly, since in the 1920s artists were mostly to be found in Montparnasse. Thus it was that I learnt the secrets of the little knoll and of the slopes below, in the footsteps of Simenon's characters, intertwined with his biography, dosed with unshrinking images from Henry Miller's *Quiet Days in Clichy*. I followed Rue Caulaincourt straddling

the cemetery in which reposes the soul of Alfred de Vigny, now in the shadow of an Ibis Hotel that did not exist in his time. I walked up Avenue Junot, not particularly receptive to the Art Deco bravura of the white houses built for Tristan Tzara and Poulbot. All in all, the dolls' houses at Villa Léandre pleased me more.

I reached Rue Norvins and lost myself in the village's black and white maze, with a marked preference for the north-facing side. The stairways of Rue du Mont-Cenis, the gardens and vineyards of Rue des Saules, the walls of Saint-Vincent cemetery, the Château des Brouillards, the Place Émile Goudeau: today, I can fill these scenic spots with figures, backdrops and situations learnt

Despite some uninteresting places, the bistros in Montmartre are generally a haven for the plain-speaking quick-witted locals, and you can still eat inexpensively in a restaurant that you come across by chance (opposite).

An old-fashioned shop, lop-sided houses, a street that leads to unknown mysteries: all are part of the unique charm that is Montmartre.

Every lover of Montmartre has his favorite slope of the hill, and even his own niche: I am particularly fond of the Rue des Saules (above).

Scale the hill by its north face, and admire the art deco houses on the Avenue Junot, before being seduced at the summit by the magic of Rue Norvins (opposite, top).

When the trees are bare and the Place du Tertre deserted, one can appreciate even more the unexpected rusticity of the uneven rows of houses (opposite, bottom).

from books. At the time, my references were not very wide. I would tail Commissioner Maigret, himself hard on the heels of some murderer or other. There were sightseers on Rue Lepic and before the portals of the church of Saint-Pierre—and a host of horrendous painters on Place du Tertre. But I had Paris in my sights—between asymmetric rooftops that somehow gave rise to unusual harmonies. The age of industry was annihilated in the commemoration of the Benedictines of yesteryear, of old-time winegrowers, of eternal insurrectionists. It was to here, I told myself, that the ever-rebellious soul of Paris fell back when the uhlan, the Nazi, or the wealthy from

Versailles laid down the law to the impoverished. Here too, the Église de France thought fit to postpone its demise by erecting a pathetic and absurd basilica. A typically bourgeois illusion: make it big, make it grand, to lure in the faithful crowds of a long-lost age. Its pseudo-Byzantinism depressed me and I was haunted by reminders of the dead Communards. Alcohol rendering such anachronisms less problematic, the memory of my patron saint spurred me to try to make the Catholic and anarchistic sides of my nature reach some kind of compromise.

I would bump into Maigret again on the Place Constantin-Pecqueur and we would tumble down the unnervingly quiet Rue Tholozé. Perhaps the murderer was eating at the famous Beauvilliers on Rue Lamarck. Or else he was on the look-out in a bar on Place Dullin whose modestly romantic theater filled me with a feeling of tenderness.

I would rejoin the boulevard which led back to Place Clichy. From there, I would lose myself in Batignolles by way of Rue des Dames. Behind the tiny white church, there stood a bar on whose pinball machine I would give vent to my anger. I have bodily lifted such machines so often—and in so many bars—that my time as a greenhorn itself resembles the breakneck careering of a metal ball let loose between the bumpers. I would return towards the bright lights by the central reservation on the Boulevard des Batignolles and roam about idly looking between Rues Pigalle and Blanche, nowhere near wealthy enough to partake of the

*T*he facade of the famous Beauvilliers restaurant brings to mind romantic suppers during the Belle Époque (opposite). Its cuisine remains as good as ever, but now has a lighter touch.

*L*ong ago, Picasso had his studio at the Bateau Lavoir. It no longer exists, but lovers still gaze into each other's eyes on the benches around the fountain (above).

scantily-clad "hostesses" who courted my libido from behind fake portholes. I too was only a fake student without a dime—I would have to find some girl who would rent out her body for free, and God knows that they were not to be found wandering around those particular streets.

There is no escape from one's childhood. Chance has ratified this psychoanalyst's axiom for me since I have often been drawn back to the area around Massillon and the Bastille. A love affair necessitated my presence in Rue de Jouy; I would purchase rare books at the Obliques bookshop on the Quai de l'Hôtel-de-Ville; I would read classic texts in the gentle half-light of the Bibliothèque de l'Arsenal; I would stock up on rock-and-roll scores at Paul Beuscher's at the end of Boulevard Beaumarchais. In addition, Simenon lived on Place des Vosges and Inspector Maigret on Boulevard Richard Lenoir. I learnt all about the Marais just as I had got to know Montmartre:

a bloodhound on the trail of a felon whose features would at least be a change from mine.

It was a district in an advanced state of disrepair. The drip-molded windows of the Hôtel de Sens, the studwork houses on the Rues François Miron and Louis-Philippe, the remains of the outer wall of Philippe Auguste behind Rue Charlemagne evoked medieval fantasies in keeping with my romanticism. The geometric rigor of the Hôtel Aumont did not fit in with the shape of my dreams, however, and it was only later that I began to admire the facade of the church of Saint-Paul, the sublime harmony of Hôtel de Sully, of the Francs-Bourgeois school, of the little dome on the church of Sainte-Marie that backed onto Rue

Tradition demands that after an evening show, elegant women and influential men dine chez Benoît, in one of the oldest streets in Paris (opposite).

No roof, no chimney, no fanlight in Paris resembles another: to inhale the poetry of this city, you must keep your nose up in the air (above).

Aesthetes do not care much for the Hôtel de Ville, fussy and heavy as it is. But no one regrets the passing of a time when public hangings were carried out on what was then Place de Grève.

36

38   *T*he birth of French seventeenth-century genius can be seen in the simple harmony of Place des Vosges, a gateway to an unreal world when the snow has fallen on the statue of Louis XIII.

Castex, a gift to the protestant church. I preferred the overflowing life of the Rue Saint-Antoine, the mysterious gleam of the blue frontage at chez Julien, the Ile Saint-Louis glimpsed from the terrace of the restaurant Louis-Philippe, the exoticism of the Jews donning their curl-papers and black bowlers on Rue des Rosiers and Rue des Ecouffes. They came from a distant land, like the Poles in Simenon's novels cooped up in the flea-ridden hotels of Rue de Birague, all providing entry to an imaginary world. Above all, I liked the idea of wandering, freely now, in the vicinity of a

school which had kept me under house arrest, astonished to discover behind Massillon a tangle of ancient streets in which a Louis XIII musketeer might have walked past a guardsman belonging to Cardinal Richelieu.

Place des Vosges—formerly Place Royale—revealed to me an aesthetic which until then I had only vaguely divined. Encapsulating a feeling for harmony, it also gave form to exaltations I owed to reading Dumas' *Three Musketeers*. Depending on my wit and whim, I could be reincarnated as Athos, D'Artagnan, or Aramis—Porthos being excluded due to his height. No backdrop could be more *musketeer* than the Place des Vosges, and the four friends did indeed meet there once during the upheavals occasioned by the Fronde, swearing an allegiance that transcended the political divide. No meeting of minds could, however, be superior to the uncomplicated marriage between its pink bricks and its running course of white stone. There is no more perfect design than the layout of its pavilion wings, of the ambulatory, and of the windows from which ladies of leisure would watch the tilting-match. The symmetric pavilions of the King and Queen provide a break in the even line of the roofing without adversely affecting the balance—and if no chimney-pot has the same shape, size, or position, the whole attains a kind of fragile perfection similar to the swooning soul at the dawn of a great love affair. It is the only place in the world where I would rather they felled the trees—three rows of limes that hide the soft-hearted yet proud simplicity of this enchanted square. For that reason, I prefer to come in the dead of winter, when the leafless boughs let one see the grille and the statue of Louis XIII—sadly not an original. If there has been snow the Place des Vosges is almost like a dreamworld: we doubt its existence, the secret of its grace has been lost for so long.

I would leave the Place by the Rue du Pas-de-la-Mule and take up my position leaning on the bar of a bistrot on Boulevard Beaumarchais. The local *bistrot de quartier* is one of Paris's many monopolies—the red lozenge sign signifying those selling tobacco. A man from Auvergne dressed in a blue apron behind the counter, a butcher boy before a large glass of white wine, a croissant basket, hard-boiled eggs and a salt-cellar, ashtrays emblazoned with the name of Ricard on the tables, Turkish toilets: there is no shortage of

How many villains have quaked on seeing the otherwise harmless tower of the judicial police headquarters as they crossed Pont Saint-Michel (opposite)? Better to retrace your steps and get caught up in the crowds around Boul'Mich.

During my youth I would cross Place des Vosges imagining I was a Musketeer and dreaming of feasts at Ma Bourgogne, unable though I was to afford them (above).

poetry in such a scene. So deep have I delved into it that a geography comprising aperitifs and digestifs overlays that of my love affairs, philosophies, and sense of architectural wonder.

I returned to the Place des Vosges with a gaze of longing, standing before the now tarnished front of the Ma Bourgogne restaurant. One day, I would say to myself without too much confidence, there'll be four of us just like the musketeers, De Gaulle will repay our work for the secret service and we'll down the dregs of many a bottle at Ma Bourgogne.

I pushed on to Rue Vieille-du-Temple and rejoined the twentieth century at the level of the Hôtel de Ville trying to picture in my mind's eye the old Place de Grève—without the overblown pastry-puff. The world below faded before the cathedral of Notre-Dame. This is the very soul of Paris, of France and perhaps of the whole world, and it has always fired my devotion. Maigret was waiting for me down by the Law Courts. His office on the Quai des Orfèvres overlooked Place Dauphine, an unfinished variation on the enchanted magic of the Place des Vosges. The trees, the benches, the sign for Restaurant Paul, like the bridge of a rudderless boat adrift on an ocean of noise and asphalt.

My pilgrimage would come to an end at the opposite end of the islands, in front of the statue of my favorite king, Henri IV, on the Pont Neuf built under his sway, and where he would venture into the anonymous crowd in the company of his friends Roquelaure and Bassompierre. The world of Simenon would dissolve, the teddy-boy in his bomber jacket would draw his rapier and land up in a brasserie on Place Saint-Michel, wondering all the while whether the long-awaited thunderstorms would, at last, dissipate the blackened sky of his melancholy.

Since then, much time has flowed beneath the bridges of the Seine. The euphoria of the 1960s has passed and the area I used to stroll in has become gentrified, trendy executives chasing out the poorer sort.

"*Paris is well worth a mass!*" *said Henri IV when he converted to Catholicism. This son of Gascony who liked good wine, easy women, and strong friendships bequeathed—to our eternal gratitude—Pont Neuf and Place Dauphine (preceding double page).*

The facade of Restaurant Paul helps to preserve my illusion that the Paris of my childhood has not changed (opposite). On Place Dauphine, time seems to stand still.

The oldest prison in Paris has housed so many of the guilty such as Ravaillac, the innocent such as Marie-Antoinette, and heroines such as Charlotte Corday that we can no longer distinguish the good from the bad (following double page).

Simenon is dead. Montmartre is a dying star, which amounts to the same thing. Around Place Pigalle, sex shops and peep-shows have ousted the time-honored ladies of the night where the red neon of a giant *Sexodrome* betrays the shift of desire towards more sordid depths: no more would the writer Francis Carco find in some bar a group of hoodlums cutting the pack with one eye on the street corner. Japanese and Dutch tourists the worse for wear may safely go without fear of being stabbed. The cabaret bar-girls snooze on their stools; it is almost at the stage that they would stump up simply to get over their boredom. At the corner of Rue André-Antoine, the brasserie Les Noctambules keeps up appearances: Paris "by night", with Pierre Carré

still producing an American version of *O sole mio*. Out-of-towners emerging from the show at Chez Michou clap without much conviction, gazing at some drag queen flat out on the bar counter like an octopus stranded on the beach. The barkeepers themselves put the decline of Pigalle firmly at the door of its takeover by the Arabs who threw out the Corsicans. They are barking up the wrong tree: it is the times that have changed, flesh is now devoured in the shape of videos, and a gangster's life is played out on screen or on the stock markets.

Montmartre is still pleasant enough in winter, late at night and especially when it is raining. Then, the mills once again stand atop the hillock and the poet Gérard de Nerval is heard

Nothing is more relaxing than the little Montmartre museum, situated in a house on Rue Cortot (opposite). The windows look out onto cottage gardens, vines, and the cemetery of Saint Vincent.

On the cobbles of Rue du Mont-Cenis, commissioner Maigret would often pursue one of the villains described by Carco, all of which adds to the charm of Montmartre (above).

In what era or in which painting by Salvador Dalì are we when we come across this orchestra of violins in Rue Elzévir? This violinist's lair, so intimate, so old-fashioned, could have been painted by Vermeer. In fact this prim little shop is in the heart of the Marais (above and opposite).

Two pavilions, "The King's" and "The Queen's", unconsciously break the symmetry of Place des Vosges, a jewel around which the Marais was built during the reign of Louis XIII (following double page).

whimpering close by the Château du Brouillard. Maurice Utrillo staggers into Rue Saint-Rustique, the novelist Marcel Aymé emerges from his tomb in the cemetery of Saint-Vincent, stirs Degas and Renoir, and rekindles the paper lanterns at the Lapin Agile for a wholly imaginary joint appearance by the oddballs from the Chat Noir cabaret and some Impressionists. Time begins to move backwards, space trips over itself. Berlioz starts composing, Gericault painting, Bruant disclaiming, Toulouse-Lautrec sketching. Place du Tertre is like a village green once again, with its cats, its local urchins, and its gaily colored shopsigns. Suzanne Valadon is there, looking for her son whom she finds seated at a table in front of a glass of absinthe.

During the day, it is less easy to imagine bygone times, though the hordes of sightseers are still restricted to the areas around the Basilica and on Place du Tertre itself. Just by descending the slopes one can inhale the plebeian Montmartre of the writers Carco, Roger Dorgelès, and Pierre MacOrlan. It smells of lilacs and country wine. One can espy the Stade de France from Rue du Mont-Cenis, the inescapable contribution of a modernity than has no sway once you enter the little museum on Rue Cortot. The windows give onto the gardens, vineyards, and the crosses of Saint-Vincent. There, too, one can admire an Utrillo quite distinct from all the others: fresher, mistier, closer to the spirit of Montmartre.

The Marais has revamped its old walls and its shopkeepers have rather overdone the fashion for "retro." Only by exploring Rue de Turenne, Rue de Sévigné, and Rue des Francs-Bourgeois is the aesthete allowed further moments of wonder: the provincial side of the Place Sainte-Catherine, the irrefutable beauty of the Musée Carnavalet, the Hôtels d'Albret and de Lamoignon. The Rue Elzévir is home to a shop belonging to a violin-maker whose panoply of instruments composes a strangely luminous symphony: and the Jerusalem monks chant sublime Gregorian at Saint-Gervais. The Marais has still more tricks up its sleeve: every time I return on the trail of memory, I glean some reminiscence of the time when the Précieuse bluestockings would go to hear the sermons of Bourdaloue at Saint-Paul, a prelude to the chaste libertinism of the boudoirs of Mlles Sévigné or Scudéry.

The Place des Victoires is just one example of how the half-century reign of Louis XIV must have been one of the most sumptuous in the history of France. The Sun King's horse rears with pride.

"You and me, Paris!"

In the end I decided to leave the city, convinced that only a conjugal farce could ever result from this marriage to Paris. The Bohemian life is costly in the long run, even in the humblest quarters, and one becomes tired of slinking around the fringes of one's ego, awaiting some improbable dawn. You are either burnt up—or you escape. Furthermore, I entertained too many misunderstandings with the century to cherish a role on the stage of History. The capital letter is deliberate: it covers those actions destined to change the world—nothing less. In the early 1970s, one had to be something of a Marxist to keep oneself amused in Paris. I was not of that persuasion, nor of any other. I was a loner. I might as well catch a train since night was always seeing me in the station bar. Farewell Paris! After nameless peregrinations, I hid myself away far out in the sticks: and, lacking as I did steady employment, the horizon of my pipedreams was vast indeed.

But France is so designed that all its railways, all its roads, all its air routes converge on Paris. It is a fatality that can be laid at the doors of our kings, further aggravated by two Empires and a succession of Republics. Ambitions and wishful thinking fester in the soft half-light of the offices

Under the arches of the Odéon theatre where the down-and-outs sleep when the weather is clement, a famous Paris publisher, Ernest Flammarion, began his career by selling books on makeshift stalls (opposite).

Marie de' Medici brought her native Florence to Paris when she built the Luxembourg palace. At the first sign of sunshine, students from the Sorbonne come to cram for their lessons in the surrounding gardens (following double page).

of all our *sous-préfets*. Sooner or later, they burgeon into an attack on the capital. Or else, they wither and die.

"You and me, Paris!" cries Balzac's Rastignac looking the unknown beauty up and down from the heights of Père-Lachaise. D'Artagnan arriving in Paris on his yellowing nag would fall prey to the same *arrivisme*. Decentralization is all well and good, but Paris is the last word for those brave hearts that burn themselves out in our sleepy provinces.

To which one should add that a man who spills ink, under whatever latitude, will always fancy associating with the shades of his illustrious predecessors in the Latin Quarter. Poets—Villon, Ronsard, Verlaine—have scattered their verse on so many street corners that their path has drawn in our hearts an invisible arabesque: one is tempted to give it one's own dose of spit and polish. So it is that, without forming the least alliance, national ambitions and vaguely metaphysical quests cross paths. The former head west, beyond the Bac–Raspail intersection, where politicians do their dirty deeds as far as Concorde, and the moneymen from there on. The latter confine themselves to the Left Bank, in an area contained within the Place Maubert, Gobelins, the Luxembourg gardens, the church of Saint-Sulpice

*T*o win over even the most reluctant, just bring them to Place Dauphine, as if nothing was happening, and invite them to lunch at the Bar du Caveau (above). The rest will follow.

*A*ll it takes is the push of a gate or a wander down a blind alley to discover a haven of rural tranquility such as Cour de Rohan (opposite).

and the Seine's two islands from whence the spirit has never ceased blowing since Lutetia took the name Paris.

I have never thought of myself as someone special, but I am so bold as to take myself for a writer. Each to his own flights of fancy! Mine claims its roots back in the rhymesters and rhetoric minds that decreed the sovereign right of Paris to rule over the kingdom of the chiseled word, the finely arranged form, and the concepts thereto accruing. In this connexion, my absence had crowned Paris with a mysteriously sensuous halo. And on occasion, when it was raining on the little town where I was living, the bliss I felt was tinged with melancholy. I would take myself off to the nearest station, I would watch the trains set off for Gare d'Austerlitz, and it dawned on me that this very word trumpeted a victory.

In the end, I boarded one. Night was falling, the suburbs were awash with light. A taxi drifted past the gates of the Jardin des Plantes, then drove by the near-gray leprosy of the Jussieu campus. The film started at the Pont Sully with the slight incurving of the Quai Béthune, the luxuriant lacework of the chevet of Notre-Dame, the sagacious asymmetry of the buildings on the Quai des Augustins, the unimpeachable classicism of the Hôtel de la Monnaie then of the Institut, the sober elegance of the facade of the Louvre, the well-ordered stream of light pouring from the lampposts on the Place de la Concorde, the heavy-handed extravagance of the Pont Alexandre III, the rigorous outlines of Les Invalides. This is the Paris of all the pictures, a mirage of haughty and unfussy perfection brought out by the luminous spangles of the *bateaux-mouches*—beyond the Trocadéro it is drowned for good, in those well-heeled quarters where one trades in the daytime and dines out at night.

The Parisian woman who invites you back remains aloof, just like those streets near the Bois (the Bois de Boulogne, that is), near Étoile, the Champ-de-Mars, or the Parc Monceau. Her offhandedness denotes the briefest fancy, not a complete surrender. One leaves her at one o'clock in the morning in the grip of some vague disenchantment. The taxi cannot make up its mind between the riverside drive and the slope of the Champs-Élysées. What are so many bright lights for if desire is at half-mast? Casting an eye over the Palais Bourbon, one finds the Greek style of the parliament building somewhat dubious. The same observation goes for the church of the Madeleine. The former Gare d'Orsay parades bourgeois lapses

When the Musée d'Orsay was a railway station the clock indicated the times of the trains, and the carved names of small towns in the Southwest on the facade were an invitation to travel.

Crossing Square Viviani, with Notre-Dame in the foreground, brings to mind what must have been the pleasant disorder of student life in the Middle Ages. All around there were schools, scholarly monks, and an abundance of taverns.

65

of taste: too much arrogance, insufficient finesse. Its great twin clocks seem to mourn some bygone dream. The carved names of small towns in the southwest inspire a desire to run away, accompanied by the scent of pastis. One discovers a single inescapable fact: Paris is a city of the North. Did the sun that made off earlier behind the gilded cupola of Les Invalides deceive us by tinting the walls blonde or pink? The city is handsome, peerless: but one can think of it lying frigid in a lonely hotel room, prey to insomnia. The dull murmur of the boulevard can be heard: Paris only sleeps fitfully, with one eye always peering into the darkness.

I took the Austerlitz train back with the feeling that someone had put one over on me. Bucolic-looking stations flew past. Cows stood in the fields, woods lay around the houses. I was delighted to return to a town where the inhabitants speak with an accent, and the doors have knockers, not entrycodes.

Seasons passed. I wrote books. Paris began to haunt me once again, if sporadically—a capricious and flighty lover, languishing by the side of her river like a diva on a sofa. I could see her in midnight blue beneath a roseate sky. I wanted to take her, to rough her up a little, to wring some

Late at night Place Vendôme is a source of much fantasy: cocktails at the Ritz bar, the display windows of Les Must de Cartier, and on one's arm an elegant lady who dreams in dollars (opposite).

The Counselors of State and members of the Constitutional Council have their offices in the Palais-Royal, but they entertain their secretaries in the booths at the Nemours (above).

67

A NOTRE

✱ I ✱ EPICERIE P. L

S¹ ANDRE DE CUBZAC
GIRONDE

C¹⁰ FEUILLADE DE CHALNA

CHATEAU TAYAC
COTES DE BOURG

S¹ SEURIN DE BOURG
GIRONDE

Mᵉ SATURNY

tears out of her at least. I took the train again, dropped my gear in one of those hotels next to Saint-Sulpice, the Pantheon or Buci frequented by foreigners if they are a touch literary. I was in the heart of Paris, hastily sampling its charms that were too overpowering to resist.

Parisian geography is simplicity itself: a center—the Latin Quarter—and outskirts that can only be reached by vast, anodyne thoroughfares laid out between the middle and the end of the nineteenth century at the behest of an all too rational bourgeoisie. The most prestigious are far from being the least nefarious: the Boulevard Saint-Michel and the Boulevard Saint-Germain chainsaw their way sadistically through the heart of student, aristocratic, and revolutionary Paris. It is sadly symbolic that they meet at the Arènes de Lutèce, close by the residence of the abbots of Cluny, admirable remains of the waning of the Middle Ages that are often left unnoticed, though the museum it houses is the most moving in all Paris.

Haussmann's supporters contend that he cleared the city by eliminating its unhealthy slums—few would disagree. The "Boul' Mich" and the Boulevard Saint-Germain nonetheless detract from the fullness of memory by concealing what we expect to see. As they are practical, people use them. The Boulevard Saint-Michel only permits a glimpse of the Pantheon, the Luxembourg Palace (side-on), the Chapelle de la Sorbonne and, at the

Not even the most ascetic could resist temptation when faced with the sumptuous display at Legrand on Rue de la Banque, just behind the Place des Victoires! (preceding double page).

The Saint-Paul district at the edge of the Marais is not cheap, but the pleasure of wandering in its tangle of little streets comes free (above).

end of the perspective, the spire of the Sainte-Chapelle.

The Boulevard Saint-Germain is scarcely more open-handed. Apart from the graceful portal of Saint-Thomas-d'Aquin (the Hôtel de Luynes having vanished), Saint-Germain's belltower and the back of Saint-Nicolas-du-Chardonnet, the only concession to the picturesque is a section of buildings between the Rue des Saint-Pères and Mabillon. I had neither the time nor the inclination to risk entering the old Paris of books on sorcery and illuminated manuscripts. Night was falling, the city was decking itself up in its bright lights. I partook of a punch in the Rhumerie, I dined at Lipp's or at Vagenende's because it was convenient and sped off west to watch the fizzling champagne bubbles and the sparkling diamonds round the female throats exposed in the bars of the grand hotels—the George V, the Crillon, the Meurice, the Ritz, the Raphael, the Bristol.

This too is a picture-postcard Paris. I would discover it in the company of some young writers who took themselves for Scott Fitzgerald. An optical illusion, plausible enough when pitching unsteadily around the Vendôme column in the dead of night. All the same, even when three sheets to the wind, I knew that the Paris of Louis XIII is more truly Parisian than that of Louis XIV. The Vendôme column is certainly voluptuous enough, but it does not win our heart. The soul of Paris is showy only when on show to the world. First thing in the morning, it floats about unbejeweled in the gaps between the more official beauties.

But how is it to be captured? I found a

The art of Renoux lies in its execution but before that there is the choice of subject matter. The Café Saint-Honoré caught his eye, and his brush creates anew a timeless Paris, a Paris that belongs to everyone.

It is wrong to believe that the charm of Paris is the prerogative of its "historical" areas. Proof of this is the Moulin de la Vierge, discovered by the artist on Boulevard Garibaldi, where the Métro travels overground (above).

Around the church of the Madeleine, wealthy ladies spend their money in the luxury delicatessens (right), before the queens of the night entice their husbands to spend theirs.

The heraldry of Paris' urchins is emblazoned on the paving stones of the Faubourg Montmartre, where the sweetmeats offered by La Mère de Famille are the least of the temptations (below).

publisher on the Rue de Richelieu. The area round the Palais Royal is not without ornament. I adored the mid-life Paris to be found on the Rue de Beaujolais where Colette used to live, on the Place des Victoires (Louis XIV again), on Rue du Mail where there was a newspaper that brought out my articles, and in the Passage Vivienne.

The publisher practised his profession in a bistrot hard by the fountain that is crowned with a statue of Molière. I jinxed him: he went bankrupt a fortnight after publishing my first book. I remain with the taste of an aborted adventure in my mouth. Then the man died. I think of him whenever I walk down Rue de Richelieu turning off the Grands Boulevards. We ate at Vieux Saumur, at Grand Colbert, or at the Brasserie Vivienne, near the passage of the same name to which he had introduced me. I used to regain the Latin Quarter by the Pont des Arts from which the night cityscape is incomparable.

I had another publisher on Place Saint-Sulpice. It took me some time to warm to this particular square, finding it conventional despite the fountain on which pigeons of an iconoclastic bent would peck at Father Bossuet's skull. To me, the church seemed ponderous and the Delacroix fresco gracing the wall to the right of the entrance seemed to go on rather. I did a little meditation before going in to correct my proofs at the Café de la Mairie and then dining at the Italian on Rue des Canettes.

Then I took to poetry—like others to religion. The Rue Princesse, Rue Guizarde, Rue des Canettes and Rue des Quatre-Vents compose a hamlet where artists and restaurant-owners address each other as *tu*. The walls have a paunch, the stores are narrow—it is yesteryear given a lick of paint, with a Mediterranean flavor when there is an international match of an evening since lovers of rugby meet up for a pint at the Bedford, at the Eden-Park or at La Bodega. The classiest people ring the bellpull at Castel's. I've downed one or two many a time, until the small hours, before returning to my hotel. Then I would go back to live and write in the countryside.

In the shadow of the columns in the Palais-Royal, the Paris tradition of plotting against the state continues (opposite).

The Bistro Vivienne has become an institution in much the same way as its neighbors: the stock exchange, the Palais-Royal, and the Bibliothèque Nationale. Money, politics, culture…and the inevitable gastronomic conclusion (following double page).

At the onset of the 1980s, chance had it that I acquired a dwelling on Rue Mouffetard. I would walk to it from the Gare d'Austerlitz, following the dark-hued buildings of the Natural History Museum on Rue Buffon. I veered off towards the Mosque whose domes and white minaret highlighted in pale green always appeared incongruous. If the weather were fine, I would go and ponder on the course of History in the Arènes de Lutèce. Heloises from the girls' campus at Censier would walk their jean-clad

Abelards, and pensioners played *boules*. Roman games had been rather more violent.

The craftsmen on "Rue Mouff" have all disappeared. In the evening, the mainly Greek restaurateurs try to harpoon the passer-by in English. The street has not lost its working-class side with its off-kilter buildings, its bars with their regulars, its market, its pretty fountain at the corner with Rue du Pot-de-Fer. One can clear one's head in the penumbra of Saint-Médard, a graceful example of late

Gothic. And there is pleasure to be had gazing at Facchetti's rustic engravings or at the mysterious shopsigns.

La Contrescarpe no longer teems with taverns, and the four trees around the fountain are railed off. But the down-and-outs still hit the bottle on the grass among the clumps of flowers, under the benign gaze of the old clock. Pigeons peck and lovers saunter, their eyes cast up at the sign "Au nègre joyeux" topped by a picture endorsing the inscription: a black man dressed like a lord taking

supper *tête-à-tête* with a society woman.

Family records attest that I spent the first year of my existence under a sloping roof on Rue Blainville. My subconscious must have pleasant recollections of it in spite of the ration cards since I feel at home in this primordial Paris—as witnessed by the Tour Clovis—to which the pupils of Henri IV and Louis-le-Grand and the students at the École Normale Supérieure and the École d'Agriculture are forever giving a new lease of life. The average I.Q. has always been high in the area around Saint-Étienne-du-Mont.

The Rue Mouffetard climbs gently up the slope of the Montagne Sainte-Geneviève, here and there displaying the charms of its great age (opposite).

Going down towards Saint-Médard, turn right: in just a few feet you have traveled from the oldest part of Paris into the quietest corner of the countryside (above).

I spent my first year of life under a roof close by the Contrescarpe. Thanks to Renoux I imagine myself back in my baby carriage, being eyed scornfully by the Nègre Joyeux, and the lamppost around which the down-and-outs continue to congregate (following double page).

*M*aybe we could all paint like Delacroix if we were lucky enough to have our studio on Place Furstenberg (above).

A moment of pleasure: go down the Rue Jacob, turn left, experience the indescribable poetry of Place Furstenberg (opposite), and admire the grace of the early baroque facade of the abbey palace.

The church itself is a light-hearted mix of Gothic and Renaissance with a hint of Baroque. Cheerfulness and distress go hand in hand: a plaque affixed to a building on Rue du Cardinal-Lemoine informs us that Hemingway stayed there, "very poor and very happy". It was during his first stay, when he wrote *A Moveable Feast*. He ate at the greasy spoons on Place Maubert and went fishing under the arches. Verlaine met his death on Rue Descartes—very poor and not very happy, though the plaque gives no further information. His funeral took place at Saint-Étienne-du-Mont, Mallarmé heading the mourning, one Symbolist replacing another.

One gets used to the Pantheon. Rue Soufflot has no savor until after

The light brown striped and varnished facade of the Allard restaurant is guaranteed to leave your mouth watering (above, top). A fine dinner at Allard has been the secret fantasy of generations of students who roam Rue Saint-André-des-Arts, seeing in themselves a latter-day Rastignac or Julien Sorel (above, bottom).

The appearance of a Morris column—or Wallace fountain—takes every Parisian back to a childhood of gazing longingly at the posters (opposite).

Directly opposite the Thermes de Cluny, the tobacconist shop Au Caïd has proudly offered an extraordinary selection of pipes for more than a century (above).

Over there, behind the church of Saint-Médard, the strangely named shop, Tuile à Loup ("wolf's roof-tile"), is just another one of Paris' many mysteries (below).

Nowadays, everything is pasteurized and we use too much canned food: this shop is a museum to modern prehistory (above).

sunset: one can see the Eiffel Tower with its orange halo behind the trees of the Luxembourg gardens. I preferred the rear of the Sorbonne and the Bibliothèque Sainte-Geneviève. The former École Polytechnique has less patina but its students learn how to be the perfect son-in-law in an institution where the spirit of finesse has the better of the spirit of geometry. Place Descartes is an oasis of rejuvenation, commemorating the time when Villon used to burglarize the Collège de Navarre that stood on the site, on the slopes of the mount of inspiration. The charm endures below on Rue de la Montagne-de-Sainte-Geneviève and down to Rue Lanneau where one can eat at the sign of the Coupe-Chou beneath the vaults of one of the oldest houses in Paris. Afterwards one can window-shop at the African bookshops on Rue des Écoles or attend a meeting at the Mutualité, the temple of left-wing consciousness which sits politely next door to Saint-Nicolas-de-Chardonnet, the sanctuary of Catholic fundamentalism. Once, out of curiosity, I wandered into each lair—the Marxist vulgate seemed to me more old-fashioned than the elaborate latin.

On the other side of the hill, the poetry is at once more provincial and less demonstrative. It was at the end of Rue Lhomond that Balzac sited the Vauquer lodging-house close to a restaurant whose terrace occupies the corner of Rue Tournefort. The atmosphere is quietly intimate, not to say adulterine. Climbing back up towards the Pantheon one crosses streets of provincial peacefulness—Rue des Irlandais, Rue Amyot—

where lawyers' houses are ensconced behind vicarage gardens. There then appears the isoceles triangle-shaped Place de l'Estrapade, like an ideal corner of some country town enfolded within the very heart of the metropolis. This, too, is Paris as Renoux sees it; moreover it was during this period that I came across his art for the first time. It was a timely discovery that rekindled childhood memories. From that time, I am always seeing myself as a schoolboy again, and I wonder whether the storekeepers are revamping their shopfronts in imitation of Renoux—or just to make me feel young once more.

You can always find the quays of the Seine at the end of a street. Charming, old-fashioned shopfronts characterize the embankments between the Boulevard Saint-Michel and the Rue Saint-Jacques.

Only a couple of steps away from the hustle and bustle of Odéon, the Saint-André passageway, cobbled as in bygone days, offers a pleasant stroll for window shoppers (opposite).

89

Rendez-vous with Verlaine

Times past, times present: above this pharmacy one can imagine Madame Pelletier as Madame Bovary, wasting away at her window.

Later on, the vicissitudes of my life as a publisher meant that my ports of call became more regular. The occasional girlfriend became the kept woman one meets with in nineteenth-century novels. Betweentimes, the publication of a number of books saw me more or less accepted as a citizen of the republic of letters. Nothing official, and of course nothing to do with the Académie. Just a slate at the bar of the "Pont-Royal" into which—its being right next to the publishers Gallimard—writers have always poured. I also obtained entry to the ground-floor of Lipp's restaurant thanks to ethnic connections with the head waiters. The preponderance of people from the Massif Central working in eateries has often earned me the special menu treatment. I pinpoint the accent, reel off some placenames and the owner stumps up a round.

My office was in front of the "Pont-Royal", on that Rue du Bac which forms the frontier between the world of letters and the world of politics, above the Maeght art gallery. I only had to cross the road and go down a few steps. The armchairs were inviting and Bernard, the barman, knew the names of every single author, be it of the slimmest volume. At the twilight of a literary life that was being eroded by television, it was comforting to drink in witty conversation with one's champagne flutes in the company of Françoise Verny or Philippe Sollers. Michel Déon would come in from Ireland, Lentz from the Ukraine or from California, Jean d'Ormesson from the Académie Française. For my part, I had come up from Corrèze where such

Chez Lipp, temple to the vanities, the pork sausage, dark beer, and headwaiters from the Auvergne are all beyond reproach.

91

On the tables at the Closerie des Lilas (opposite), plaques commemorate regulars such as Hemingway, Aragon, Beckett and even Lenin. The pianist hails from a later era but the ambiance evokes that of Montparnasse in the good old days.

The ludicrous style of the Bistro de la Gare is a reminder of what we have lost (above). Montparnasse no longer has its railway station, its painters, and its good-time girls all the way from Brittany. All that remains is the pancake houses.

literary tournaments would see supporters of an open game doing battle with those who favored a more attritional rugby.

I would meet up with François Nourissier and Pierre Chaunu at Lipp's. They spoke to me of a time when an article by Jean-Paul Sartre, composed on a bar-bench at the Deux Magots, would panic a government. I sipped brown ale conjuring images of an existentialist or jazz-filled Saint-Germain-des-Prés that no longer survives. "Too late", I would murmur to myself climbing towards Rue Mouffetard through a Rue Jacob saturated with antique shops.

I would bump into Antoine Blondin who would always mix me up with one of the hookers playing for Tarbes R.F.C.—or else with a poet who had been dead twenty years. I walked him back to his rat-trap on Rue Mazarine. A final glass at the Rubens, in a bar that has since vanished as has the Pont-Royal. Blondin is dead. The fonder of Paris I became, the more I would curse it for warbling the same old nostalgic songs.

In the end I took student digs in a street near the chapel of Val-de-Grâce where Anne of Austria came to plot against Richelieu with the Spanish priests. The facade and dome of the building itself

A glass of poetry and a dose of exotica is what you get at the Molay. This café that roasts its own coffee looks out onto the Odéon theater (above).

You don't have to be an artist or a politician to be famous in Paris, the baker Lionel Poilâne is proof of that: no other bread comes close to his (opposite).

*Generations of impecunious
students have crossed the
threshold of Polidor where one
can eat well for next to nothing.
Just next door is where Whistler
painted his portrait of Robert de
Montesquiou.*

96

connived to evolve my aesthetic: I began to recognize the merits of its restrained classicism, both subtle and invigorating. On the strength of it, I went on to re-evaluate the Chapelle de la Sorbonne, the facade of the Institut, the dome of Saint-Paul—everything that the French genius had derived from early Italian Baroque.

I was in that age-old and wretched quarter, cut in two by an ancient Roman road. It appears that Jean de Meung wrote the *Roman de la Rose* in the Rue Saint-Jacques, and it is always touching to feel the Middle Ages peeking up from beneath the asphalt. My publisher lived on the top story of his building. His bay window looked down over the roofs, a gray or bluish zinc maelstrom of tiles, slate, and chimney stacks. If they date from the same period, the walls of Paris are all much the same; each roof, however, is different depending on its pitch, its materials, the shape of its balcony, its chimney pots, its transoms and even its gutter-trough. You

have to walk along with your nose pointing skywards, or else live beneath the eaves, to gain entrance to the intimacy of all those thousands of little villages cooped up beneath the rafters.

So close to the Port-Royal crossroads, I could hardly miss the Closerie des Lilas in front of which the Second Empire erected a statue of Field Marshal Ney, a homage he amply deserves. The epoch of Bullier dances ended donkeys' years ago, but the memory lives on at the bar of La Closerie. There I would meet Hallier, whose eloquence was most diverting. He would all of a sudden take off to foil some improbable plot or other and I would find myself alone with famous men long since dead and buried, whose names were inscribed on the plaques fixed onto the tables: Hemingway, Aragon, Modigliani, Lenin....

I would only go to Montparnasse to eat stuffed crab at the Créole, pig's ears at the Coupole or else to stroll amongst the tombs in the

*T*imes change: while Café Flore has remained an important meeting place for political and journalistic bigwigs (above), nowadays they meet around a basket of croissants, the working breakfast being the current fashion.

*T*he waiters at the Flore know their clientele and tables are allocated, among other criteria, according to political allegiances. They know the secrets of those demi-gods that make up the Paris elite (opposite).

cemetery. My publishing house set up camp for a year on Rue Huysmans. I searched vainly for the spirit of Montparnasse around the Boulevard since rendered nondescript by tourism. The Carrefour Vavin has kept something of its Bohemianism with the law students from Rue d'Assas at tables on the terrace, but there are no artists' studios on Rue Delambre and the Gaité looks more like Pigalle with its sex shops and its shady saunas. I would often take a coffee first thing in a brasserie on Boulevard Port Royal with Sollers who would hold forth in scholarly tones on libertinage, on Voltaire, or on Situationism. Every Parisian intellectual has an -ism or two up his sleeve. I am rather more a libertarian than a libertine and not Voltairian in the least, but I enjoy denigrating the society of the spectacle while helping myself to warm croissants. Paris has a genius for croissants, for the *baguette* and for intellectual blabla, alluring and worthless.

Sollers could lay bare the pitfalls of his caste for all he was worth, his colloquys remained firmly in the tradition of salon chitchat between well-behaved literary types: he is possessed of *esprit*, of culture and has the art of the well-judged and skillfully weighted paradox that is the hallmark of those who haunt the banks of the Seine.

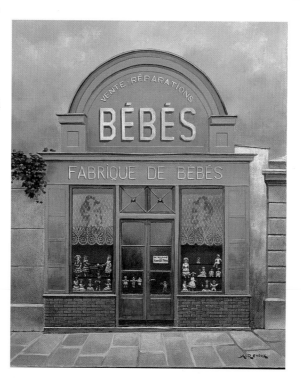

A surrealist insight or the premonition of a soothsayer? This strange shop, alas now demolished, might have been the setting for some geneticist's nightmare.

At nighttime, I plunged into the Rue du Faubourg-Saint-Jacques, returned back up the Boulevard Blanqui under the metal armature of the overhead subway and climbed Rue Barrault to half-way up the slope of the Butte des Cailles. There stood a connoisseur's bookshop whose owner, recently emerged from the most unyielding anarchism, could dig out unknown and obscure writers: Calet, Guerin, Vialatte. With chilling irony, it is Calet who depicts a fourteenth *arrondissement* full of pensioners close in spirit to the twelfth in which I started out.

Viewed from a distance, or from the distant past, all these areas that burgeoned in the industrial era look the same. One needs time and tenderness to pinpoint just what makes each different. Rue Hallé, which I adore, is like no other: one would think oneself in George Sand's county of Berry.

The ultra-revolutionaries that hung out in this bookstore drowned their disillusionment in literary fervor. A most respectable surrogate. We would climb back up to the top of the hill and lay into a hearty meal downed with some rough red wine while dissecting the stylistic merits of Forton, Gadenne, and other unheard-of writers. Drunkenness tended to revive their dreams of insurgency and I was put in mind of wordy nights spent in spring 1968. But History never serves us the same dish twice and we must remain orphans of our youthful enthusiasms. This was true of them more than of myself as wine made it no easier to mount the barricades. It would

Everyone knows Montmartre, Montparnasse, the Montagne Saint-Geneviève, and the Buttes Chaumont. But few know the Butte aux Cailles, a delightful hillock which in some parts has retained its village-like charm.

all the more easily accord me a reprieve from dreams *à la* Rimbaud, since the revolt of which I dream still (struggle against it though I might) is not to be found inscribed in the historical inventories of a city set aflame by some Étienne Marcel or ersatz Cohn-Bendit.

More years passed by. My relationship to Paris was as changeable as the sky over Ireland: first rainy, then ecstatic. Without speaking of maturity exactly, I had reached the stage at which, prior to consuming hungrily one's heart's desire, one takes time out to reflect upon it.

I was installed behind the Carrefour de l'Odéon where the statue of Danton and an unremittingly malfunctioning clock regiments a host of invisible village corners. The soaring growth of banking establishments and rag-trade outlets on Boulevard Saint-Germain has not destroyed the graces of an *arrondissement*—the sixth—where the ghost of a writer, a musician, a painter, or a ne'er-do-well is forever bumping into that eminently Parisian personage, the intellectual. The latter may be identified by his corduroy trousers, his thick-rimmed spectacles, his esoteric jargon, and his progressive theories. He has come out of the Sorbonne, the Collège de France or the Lycée Saint-Louis or else from some publishing office to take lunch at the Balzar—the Lipp for the studious—which preserves its Art Deco interior intact. Or perhaps he invites a pretty student to some trendy art house cinema such as Champollion or Racine's on Rue de l'École-de-Médecine.

In this narrow bottleneck, one simply has to push a door ajar to be able to admire the six-sided cupola of the former lecture hall—dating from the Grand Siècle—near the disaffected Franciscan Abbey in which Danton spewed forth his Roman Republic sentiments before they guillotined him. One is well within one's rights to excoriate the quadruple colonnade that serves as an overture to the School of Medicine itself with its statue of Bichat, and deplore the disappearance of the house in which Baudelaire saw the light of day in the Rue de Hautefeuille, on the rubble of a former Jewish cemetery. But the shades of Baudelaire are ever-present, communing on the two infinities with those of Pascal who himself had brought his ideas to maturity in the upper reaches of Rue Monsieur-le-Prince.

A perfect miniature of the aesthetic that was the genius of the French seventeenth-century: this doorway on Rue Monsieur-le-Prince, sculpted out of pale stone, incorporates an extravagantly coiffed cherub.

Between the river and Boulevard Saint-Germain Rue des Saints-Pères offers a selection of luxury shops. It is also the antique dealers' square mile.

105

It is a street for all tastes. The aesthete faints with rapture before the molding on a portal at the entrance to Rue Dupuytren. For those on the lookout for company, one can always chat up a young girl from the Sorbonne at Polidor's whose frontage has remained unaltered since the Belle Époque, just like that of Bouillon Chartier's on Rue Racine, now converted to a restaurant for Belgian cuisine.

It is only to the pedestrian that Paris is truly open. It was for that very reason that I positioned my publishing house on the short Rue Corneille where Balzac had lodged Z. Zarkas. That fervent youth scorched his wings in the flaming candle of politics. The senators one encounters in this neck of the woods, however—on a break from the gilt halls of the Palais du Luxembourg—have no more wings to burn. They dine with their mistress at La Méditerranée whose frescoes have witnessed the comings-and-goings of the great and the good of several Republics. At twilight, when the beige walls on the Place de l'Odéon veer to orange, the sudden appearance between the columns of the theater of the kind of little figures Watteau would paint is not uncommon. Under the arches now invaded by tramps, Ernest Flammarion had his bookshop before he went on to found his publishing house on Rue Racine. The area has always been a place for intellectuals. Mallarmé and the Symbolists were regulars at the Voltaire, on the corner of that selfsame Rue Racine. Adrienne Monnier and Sylvia Beach would receive Hemingway, Eliot, or Joyce in their bookstores on Rue de l'Odéon and later it was here that Cioran was to concoct his aphorisms and Régis Debray his dreams of a virtuous and martial republic. I swapped ideas with him —and a few of his colleagues—in a bookstore where they would gather to cast the world anew—a thing much needed. It too was to be foundon the Rue de l'Odéon. So it was that the spirit of bookstores such as Amis des Livres and Shakespeare and Co. had not died a death, though this goes against the flow in that the period was one of waning influence for bookshops.

Athos, the romantic hero of Alexandre Dumas' Three Musketeers, *lived in Rue Férou, with just the right amount of shade and the towers of Saint-Sulpice rising forth. Behind the walls of the private mansions are suitable settings for all kinds of insurrection (opposite).*

Casanova resided in Rue de Tournon. No doubt he would have liked to pick up some of the pupils attending dancing classes chez George, or to add to the sum of his knowledge in this antiquarian bookshop (following double page).

Parisians entertain an affection for the Luxembourg gardens that comes from their having been short-trousered freshwater boatmen: all have at one time launched a little sailboat onto the ornamental lake. Having been anchored rather in open country, I can only dismiss out of hand the rusticity of these trees and herbaceous borders railed off like the jailbirds in the Prison de la Santé. Even the Palace gets my goat. It apes Florence and I loathe Marie de'Medici—bad wife, bad mother, bad Regent, and moreover, ugly. Rubens wasted his efforts trying to idealize her, and his allegorical saga in the Louvre is wearisome.

On the other hand, I do like the bars that run along outside the garden. The Petit Suisse, outside which girls from the university sunbathe in the warmer season; the Rostand from which can be espied the Médicis fountain; the Tournon used by the office-workers from the Sénat. Poor Joseph Roth stayed there. The Renaissance poet Clément Marot and Casanova occupied the same town house on Rue de Tournon, near to the Cours George and to an antiquarian bookshop whose shopfront is not devoid of character.

Two other self-effacing streets descend towards Saint-Sulpice, Rue Servandoni and Rue Férou, where Athos resided in the *Three Musketeers*. They get mixed up in my brain, as does Rue Canivet that links them and which perhaps terminates in Rue Bertrand-de-Jouvenel, as a four-numbered homage to a thinker from Corrèze. Or was it there that Faulkner passed through at the same time as Hemingway and Gertrude Stein? Or is it the site of the restaurant Saint Pourçain whose house wine, served chilled, catapults one back into the reign of Louis XIII? This is the Paris one dreams of when reading Dumas: high walls, carriage doors, cobblestones.... Could the petticoat leaving through that portal adorned with sphinxes belong perhaps to Constance Bonacieux? The curtain drawn at the window of some residence— is that the Duchesse de Chevreuse? She is waiting for Aramis who lived on Rue de Vaugirard. Or for an emissary from the Duke of Buckingham. A clatter of hooves approaches, a swordblade gleams in the light of a torch, a shadow projects from the house backing onto the apse of Saint-Sulpice, whose towers become evermore religious in the graceful bluish radiance.

A final glass *chez* Lipp? One can hardly bring oneself to believe that Porthos lived in Rue du Vieux-Colombier. The music of Claude Luter

A clatter of hooves, a clash of swords. A king's musketeer duels with one of Richelieu's guards in the Rue Férou, outside the home of a duchess as she trembles with fear and joy.

and Sydney Bechet no longer makes the walls swing, and one has to cross the yawning chasm that is the Rue de Rennes to meet up once more with the Paris of the duchesses in the Rue Bernard de Palissy. The fires of existentialism are extinguished around the belltower that mourns the poets Jules Supervielle and Max Jacob, or Jean-Paul Sartre and Antoine Blondin. I can well recall the obsequies they held for Blondin; there were few writers and too many hangers-on getting a thrill from his legendary status as a barfly. One for the road at the Danton. It is the last brasserie open. Monsieur Aguigui or Professor Choron stop off there on occasion to renew their acquaintance with tall stories and utopian dreams in the tradition of Ferdinand Lop.

Out of cigarettes. Since the Drugstore closed down, there is only one all-night tobacconist, on the Boulevard Saint-Michel. The boss is from the Aveyron, just as he should be. The desperadoes that patrol in front of the fountain on Place Saint-Michel, short of hash or cocaine, come from nowhere at all. Back to the Odéon by way of Rue Suger where I have seen beams with seventeenth-century paintings in a friend's apartment. Suffice it to say that this stretch of town was not born yesterday, a fact proclaimed loud and clear by the turret emerging from Rue Hautefeuille. The clock says midnight—but it's wrong.

The last bus has gone, the last cinema has shut its doors. The night has to be faced and one can tell oneself that even Verlaine felt lonely when he left the Procope.

Supper at the Procope, the oldest café in Paris, will bring you into contact with the traditional French art of speaking eloquently without actually saying anything, in the company of Voltaire, Diderot, d'Alembert, and other men of letters. Personally I would prefer to get drunk with Alfred de Musset.

Peaceful Paris Days

It is no easy task to ford the divide that separates the two sides of the Boulevard Saint-Germain. It took me years to break the ties that bound me to the Théâtre de l'Odéon and forge my way as far as the Seine. Unconsciously, I was treating Paris as one might a wife—fitfully though fully aware of her attributes. I would reach the *quais* by way of Rue Dauphine or to the Pont-Royal by Rue Jacob. Paris, however, is a mistress, not a wife, and she clams up when she feels she is being embraced with one eye on the clock.

This I duly noted. It was traipsing around—only a hundred yards from where I lived—that I came across the arcade of the Passage de Saint-André and the delectable Cour de Rohan sheltering beneath its vaulted roof, just opposite the Procope whose gilded wainscot, chandeliers, fake leather benches, and medallions are suggestive of somewhat high-brow junketing. It was by chance that a friendship brought me onto the Place Furstenberg near which I must have walked a hundred times without once encountering it, though the abbot's palace is a prime example of my preferred style, a typically French miracle of the kind of grace, divine yet as simple as ABC, which held sway between the rule of Henri III and Louis XIII. Around the lampstand with its five globes and the four trees—two still saplings—the white walls and the roofs have contrived a bucolic phantasmagoria whose lyricism wafts up as far as Rue Cardinale. At the first tight bend is a two-windowed house adorned with a wrought-iron balcony and a Virginia creeper. One dreams of writing a book in that house.

One might dream of writing another in the sublime *hôtel* on Rue des Grands-Augustins in which Balzac placed the plot of the *Chef d'œuvre inconnu*. Picasso painted *Guernica* here. Opposite, Louis XIII was enthroned as a child an hour after

The enchantment which comes over one on Place de Furstenberg continues into the network of tiny streets which join up with Boulevard Saint-Germain at the Mabillon intersection.

In Rue Dauphine, there are hidden courtyards that resemble trompe-l'œil paintings in the style of de Chirico (above).

Does tea-drinking lead to marriage? This lovely reader seated at a table in Mariage Frères, in an atmosphere redolent of Hopper, highlights the play on words (opposite).

his father Henri IV had been fatally stabbed by an extremist—for they existed even at that time. The Paris of the late Valois kings and the following two centuries with their four Louis comes back to life and marries with the modern world as I remember it in a tangle of windows with guttering and spick-and-span shopfronts. The brown-varnished, black-streaked wood of Restaurant Allard, the lighter chestnut of the Mariage Frères store ("all blends of tea"), the graffiti left by medics at Jo la Grenouille's are the offspring of the Tour de Nesle that served as the Parisians' Eiffel Tower in former times, and the escapades of Reine Margot who started the whole fashion for the quarter by, it is said, throwing her lovers into the Seine.

At the end of every street, one will always find the *quais*. I took up the habit of going in beneath each porch. Both the Renaissance and the Grand Siècle have bequeathed mansions here that can broach comparison with those of the Quai d'Anjou. I went back to my old custom of lingering in front of the green bookseller structures of the *bouquinistes*. They are still as they always have been, with an unhindered view of the apse of Notre-Dame. I crossed over Place Saint-Michel and came within range of another village, beyond Saint-Julien-le-Pauvre and Saint-Séverin. Primitive Romanesque or full-blown Gothic? My preference would always run to the Romanesque, I pondered, as I crossed the Square Viviani where Master Albert Magnus's clerks used to keep up the dispute concerning Universals. Those customers at Shakespeare and Co. on Place du Petit-Pont have quite other universal concepts in mind.

I am not sure whether this too is Sylvia Beach's responsibility, like its namesake on Rue de l'Odéon—and I am never able to recollect the

Every time I pass the Italian restaurant on Rue du Cherche-Midi I am hailed by a famous actor who has set up home there as have many others, and we drink to the health of our fellow rugbymen.

119

quotation from Walt Whitman whose portrait serves as its shopsign—but in the picture archives of my mind I retain a cameo of this cramped bookstore as the kind of medieval shop that must have existed when Paris was a fragmented village.

Still under the eye of the rose-window of Notre-Dame, I continue my stroll through minute and nameless squares between Quai Montebello and Quai de la Tournelle, from the start of Rue de la Bûcherie and Rue de Bièvre, the latter long under police surveillance since it was the home of President Mitterrand. Rue Hôtel-Colbert; Rue du Haut-Pavé; Rue des Grands-Degrés—like a sequence of sea ports, with, at the quayside, barges transformed into restaurants where I often while away the hours.

Here I am, back on the Ile de la Cité. I take the time to visit the Sainte-Chapelle. This is the medieval France of valiant knights and pious men whose soul still sighs quietly from riverbank to riverbank, only slightly overshadowed by the ponderous central law courts—the Palais de Justice, and the general hospital—Hôtel-Dieu.

Its spirit lives on in the mansion on Rue Chanoinesse that looks onto the Quai aux Fleurs. At night, as one slides past the towers of the Conciergerie prison, one can almost hear it sigh. This echo melds with that of the martyrs deported during the War, rising from the crypt dedicated to their memory at the end of the square behind Notre-Dame. The architect has captured the mechanisms of imprisonment through his use of iron. Why are there so many crimes? The Quai d'Orléans is so cool, so calm, that one cannot imagine how evil could ever be permitted to take root there. Vercors lived on this *quai*, not far from the footbridge that links the two islands and I recall meeting him shortly before his death to talk about the Resistance. The place is conducive to doing so: "Paris violated" and "Paris liberated," as they used to say. The *Te Deum* of the Liberation has added the conduct of General de Gaulle to the memorable list of noble deeds and jubilatory acts celebrated in Notre-Dame.

Though never in a professional capacity, there was a time when I would patrol up and down the

Behind Notre-Dame, in Rue Chanoinesse looking out onto the Seine, there are superb mansions that date back to the Renaissance (opposite).

Notre-Dame remains the jewel in the crown of this queen of cities. It is the soul of Paris, witness to its failures, its exploits, and its mourning, as well as the apotheosis of Gothic art (following double page).

frontiers of politics. One is always dreaming of instilling something of the ideal into reality, above all in this city that has so regularly served as a theater for the destiny of man. Revolutions, restorations, liberations, uprisings spawned by utopias, fostered by anger, encapsulated forever in a witticism or in an act of bravura: Notre-Dame has seen the good, the bad, and the ugly.

I myself have only seen some insignificant barons beneath the glass chandeliers that hang in a few state palaces. And that, thankfully, not for long since one soon wearies of it all. I can see myself now, in the President's Elysée Palace, at the Prime Minister's residence at Matignon, at the Chancellor's Office, at the Foreign Office on the Quai d'Orsay, at the Hôtel de Lassay or at the Luxembourg Palace, as if I were the fool in some inferior period drama taking place in interiors that I have a tendency to mix up. All prisons are much of a muchness, however ornate they are. The Parc de Matignon is the grandest, the cooking at the Quai d'Orsay is fine, and the library at the Luxembourg palace would have enchanted Borges—that is about all I can remember.

The majority of Paris's ministries being situated in the old area of Saint-Germain, I learnt to distinguish between Rue de Varenne, Rue de Grenelle, and Rue Saint-Dominique. They are as alike as the well-behaved children in the morality

For three generations, prosperous Parisians have chosen to live in the sixteenth arrondissement. A certain amount of character has managed to seep in between the luxury apartment blocks, such as this local grocery store.

When one leaves the Maison de la Radio, not in itself a particularly attractive building, one longs for a little human warmth in an old fashioned café-bar (above).

Rigorous, simple, unaffected: such are the secrets of what is known as French elegance, developed between the seventeenth century and the Enlightenment, and shown here by these sculpted pediments (following double page).

novels of the Comtesse de Ségur. The architecture of the various mansions dates from some Louis or other and they are majestic enough. If I were a foreigner on my way through, I would surely take a walk around them, but they fall short on atmosphere. Such *ennui* hovers over Sainte-Clotilde that one could hardly summon up the energy to debauch one of its parishioners—even supposing one had the means.

Beyond, there stretches a coldly silk-stockinged city, arranged in lines as straight as a die around the Champ-de-Mars, Les Invalides, and the École-Militaire. Blondin wrote thus: "Past nine in the evening, heroes with a thirst for adventure are not be met with in the streets around Les Invalides." I have never encountered one of a morning either, and my aversion to the seventh *arrondissement* extends to the eighth (Rue de Rome excepted), the sixteenth (apart from Auteuil, and Le Stella and Le Passy of the overhead Métro) and the seventeenth (save for Batignolles). The day my publisher departed from Saint-Sulpice to set up shop on Rue Marceau I was tempted to change him—and if I enjoy lunching *chez* Edgar on Rue Mabeuf it is only so as to be able hear what no pressman would dare print. During my forays amongst our political friends, I had been assigned chambers in Rue Pérouse near Étoile. The closeness of the house in which De Gaulle had taken up residence following the Liberation did not of itself make the place any more bearable. I would have opted instead for an attic-room under some roof in Paris, by which I mean in the real Paris, the one with corpses buried under the paving stones. I would walk home along the Champs-Élysées and, though I would think of Proust, I still felt like an exile until reaching the top of the Quai Voltaire whose length I used to pace as a student in the hope of bumping into Montherlant. Beyond the demarcation line of the Rue du Bac, from the Bon Marché department store to Pont-Royal, I will always feel like an alien longing for a visa.

Henceforth, Paris will have nothing but secrets for me which it will reveal when I emerge from the most far-flung Métro stations. Once it downs its "classic" mask, its stiff collars, and Belle Époque greasepaint, this Atlantis of the venerable North proves itself the labyrinth of all our desires, the kaleidoscope of all our pipedreams.

The demiurge sculpted above this doorway on Rue Saint-Roch resembles Napoleon who used to live in this highly insurrectionary quarter.

*T*he Procope has been
perfectly restored to its former
style. Almost too perfectly:
everything is so correct that a
modern-day bohemian feels just
a little out of place here. But
the mark of time will remedy
that, and some future Verlaine
will no doubt come here to
misbehave and leave traces of
his poetry and wine on the
tablecloths.

We will never live together because her nerves are too on edge. She slackens them a notch whenever there is the prospect of nightly pleasure, when she dons her finest and smiles into her looking-glass framed in beige stone. Or else first thing in the morning, when the sound of the percolator behind a gleaming bar sets the scene for the indescribable sensuousness of that first cigarette. Ah! a typist's red lipstick on the filter of her first Marlboro cigarette of the morning!

Independent, provocative, languorous, bewitching—Paris can fulfill any role—save that of a full-time lady companion. In daylight, she dozes or works herself up in her all too broad avenues that have ordered the city too rationally, leaving scant room for superlatives. Night camouflages the crimes committed by Haussmann and his apostles in the name of city planning, just as unsightly as those dating from after the War—the Jussieu campus, the École de Médecine on Rue des Saints-Pères, the Maison de l'ORTF housing the French broadcasting corporation, the Beaubourg arts' center, the Tour Montparnasse, Beaugrenelle, and the heights of Belleville and Ménilmontant. Should the votaries of Bercy and La Défense be exonerated? Let us concede that offices to contain executives and telephones are necessary, that one has to "live with one's time", though the expression, the diktat, remains a controversial one.

Setting aside the respect due to André Malraux and his new broom, modernism has proved at once heavy-handed and awkward. Squares have been renovated, it is true, and our monuments have been bedecked in lights, while behind Montparnasse the architect Ricardo Bofill has done much better than he might. But Paris could have well done without all the rest. Modernity suits New York, Berlin, and Singapore. Beneath the bridges of the Seine it is a history lost in the mists of time that flows along. We desire Venice at some period between the century of Titian and that of Canaletto. St Petersburg will always live its life in the age of Peter the Great, Vienna at the time of Sissi, an archduke, and a Strauss waltz. Istanbul is Pierre Loti's Orient, and London, the carriage of Queen Victoria.

Whereas Paris, in accordance with our whims, can reconstitute itself from its past. The coffee-roasters on Rue Crébillon or the Tuile à Loup on Rue Daubenton, so dear to Renoux, emerge from the depths of time that aggrandizes them just as much as it does the ogives of Saint-Eustache or the

Up there, under the rooftops, the maid had her room. Monsieur had the key, but Madame was unaware, and the class struggle was forgotten in an embrace, enacted under the watchful eye of a Morris column.

My compatriots from the Auvergne and the Corrèze have been unrivaled masters of the wood, coal, and café trades for over a century. They have worked their way into every district, even those around the Gare de l'Est.

arches of the Pont-Neuf. The arcades of the Rue de Rivoli, of the Palais-Royal, and of the Théâtre de l'Odéon blend into a single secluded passage through which pass the characters in our script.

I will always meet up with my various alter egos at the crossroads of memory. They persist in drifting off towards Daumesnil, round the zoological gardens, and the Museum dedicated to our late colonies. I am indebted to the crocodiles in the tank, the carved elephants on the frieze, and the wolves hemmed in behind their railings for a precocious yearning for the jungle, the desert, and the savannah, that is, for the antipodes of that world that grown-ups were already dubbing "modern" in the mid-1950s. Not far away, near the "Cipale"—the oval cycling stadium—which was built at the same time, and entertains a similar nostalgia, the former Togo and Cameroon pavilions act as props to the unfocussed exoticism of those rambles that fascinate me so much.

Here I am once again hand-in-glove with the Paris of the street arabs, the rough-and-ready Paris of hotels with no stars ("running water on all floors"), whose churches are not even mentioned in the guide-books: Notre-Dame-de-Lorette down at the end of Rue des Martyrs, Sainte-Marguerite next to Charonne, or Jeanne-d'Arc behind the "Très Grande Bibliothèque." I still feel the same attraction for the Saint-Martin canal where the Hôtel du Nord was unearthed, for the Pont Cardinet—an invisible checkpoint dividing the Paris of the rich from that of the poor—for the tombs in Père-Lachaise, for the unhinged temple in the Buttes Chaumont gardens, for the bistrots in Belleville and the stalls of Ménilmontant. Each new foray relieves me of yet another corner of paradise caught up in hell. Those houses on Rue Irénée-Blanc behind Boulevard Mortier are the dream of a pensioner who wants to see out his days in the countryside. This habitation, recaptured by the followers of Jean Dubuffet, at the bottom of a garden behind Rue de Sèvres, is the perfect place for a lawyer to hide his girlfriend. These chalets stuck in three little streets side-on to the Parc Montsouris are an ideal holiday resort in miniature. The lanes with the names of their "villas" in which one finds naively striped maisonettes in miniature around the Danube Métro station give a glimpse of San Francisco. One can travel from Asia at the Porte de Choisy, to Africa at Barbès, and clear one's mind as the rain patters on the roofs. The pleasant, semi-circular park at Balard backing onto the railroad track, is the Paris of Doisneau, that of my childhood. It has not disappeared, I find it still untouched on the Ile Saint-Louis towpath, under the chiseled arcades of the Place des Vosges, in the vines of Rue Cortot, around Saint-Étienne-du-Mont. "The shape of a city," wrote Baudelaire, "changes faster than the heart of mortal man." So it does, more's the pity. And I would prefer it if Paris were to lend itself more to repetition and less to innovation. Crossing the Jardin des Plantes, I sometimes catch sight of the clock-tower of the Gare de Lyon, now dwarfed between two pale modern blocks, and I realise how ephemeral it all is: at one time the clock-tower could be seen from miles away. But the city harbors a secret of eternal life to outfox all the developers. You just have to be in love to stop the sands of time flowing at dusk and set sail into the endless night, as if straddling a cloud on its way to heaven. Paris is a state of mind, a voluptuous asceticism, a homage to capriciousness, a search warrant for life, carved out by memory and sung by the wind that gently swirls across the Seine.

The down-and-outs of Rue Saint-Louis-en-l'Ile have been replaced by tourists. But it has retained its traditional shops. This butcher is considered one of the best in Paris (above).

*S*imone Signoret and Yves Montand lived behind these windows on Place Dauphine, which can be glimpsed through the trees and the lawyers' gowns (above).

*I*n another life, God willing, I would happily be an innkeeper opposite Notre-Dame, and from time to time take a barge back to the forests of my beloved Corrèze (following double page).

André Renoux's
Paris

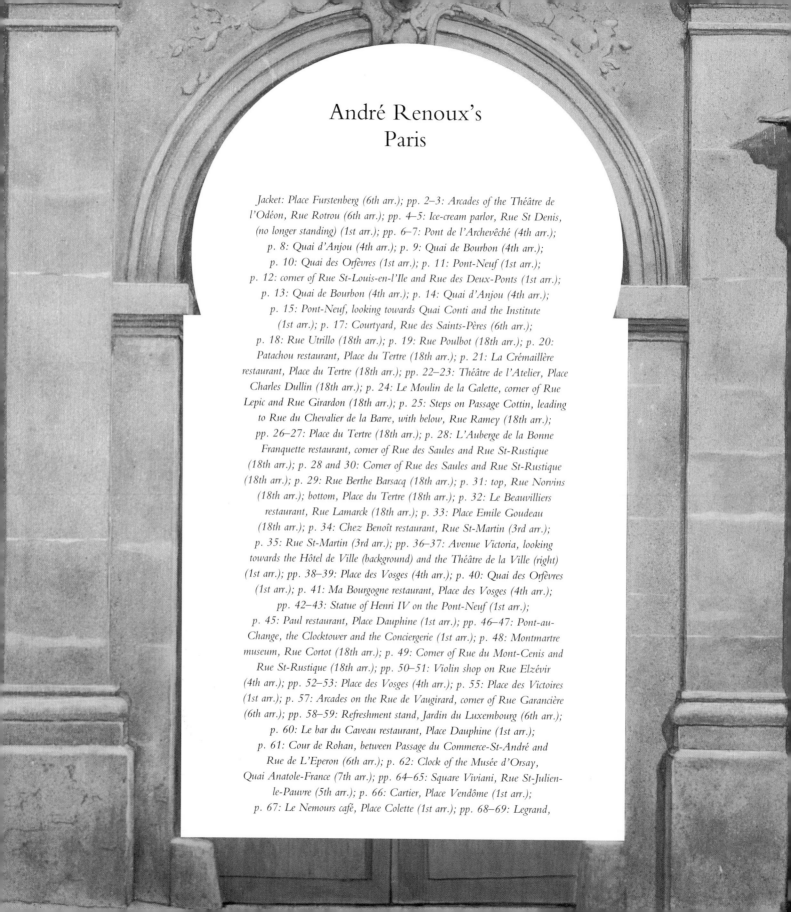

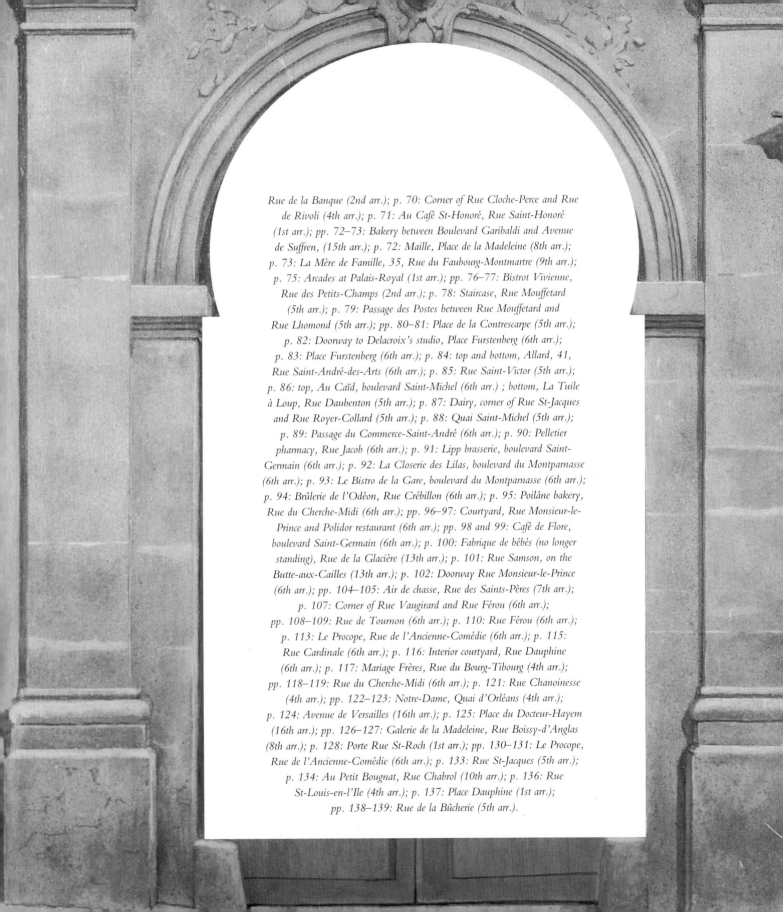

Works by
André Renoux

André Renoux Paris, text by Bernard Dimey,
(ABC/André Roussard, 1979).

New York by Renoux, text by Christopher Robinson,
(Éditions André Roussard, 1984).

André Renoux Paris, text by Bernard Dimey,
preface by Jean-Edern Hallier, (Éditions Jean Picollec/André
Roussard, 1987) (published in English as *Paris by Renoux*,
currently out of print).

Works by André Renoux are also reproduced
in the following publications:

Paris vu par les peintres de Corot et Foujita,
(Éditions du Musée Carnavalet, 1978).

Amélie Chazelles, *Montmartre vu par les peintres,*
preface by Claude Charpentier, (Edita, 1988).

Sylvie Buisson, *Les Peintres de Notre-Dame-de-Paris,*
(Éditions Conti, 1990).

Works by
Denis Tillinac

Le Rêveur d'Amériques, (Paris: Robert Laffont, 1980).

Le Mystère Simenon, (Paris: Calmann-Lévy, 1980).

Le Bonheur à Souillac, (Paris: Robert Laffont, 1982) (Prix libre, Prix de la Table Ronde française).

L'Été anglais, (Paris: Robert Laffont, 1983) (Prix Roger Nimier).

A la santé des conquérants, (Paris: Robert Laffont, 1984).

Spleen à Daumesnil, and *Le Tour des îles*, (Le Dilettante, 1985).

L'Ange du désordre, Marie de Rohan, duchesse de Chevreuse, (Pairs: Robert Laffont, 1985).

Spleen en Corrèze, (Paris: Robert Laffont, 1985).

Vichy, (Champ Vallon, 1986).

L'Irlandaise de Dakar, (Paris: Robert Laffont, 1986).

Maisons de famille, (Paris: Robert Laffont, 1987) (Prix Kléber-Haedens).

Un léger malentendu, (Paris: Robert Laffont, 1988).

Le Bar des palmistes, (Arléa, 1989).

La Corrèze et le Zambèze, (Paris: Robert Laffont, 1990) (Prix Jacques-Chardonne).

L'Hôtel de Kaolack, (Paris: Robert Laffont, 1991).

Les Corréziens, with Pierre Dauzier, (Paris: Robert Laffont, 1991).

Le Retour de d'Artagnan, (Paris: La Table Ronde, 1992).

Rugby blues, Paris: La Table Ronde, 1993) (Prix populiste, 1993; Grand Prix de la littérature sportive, 1994).

Le Jeu et la chandelle, (Paris: Robert Laffont, 1994).

Dernier verre au Danton, (Paris: Robert Laffont, 1996).

Elvis, balade sudiste, (Paris: La Table Ronde, 1996).

Don Juan, (Paris: Robert Laffont, 1998).

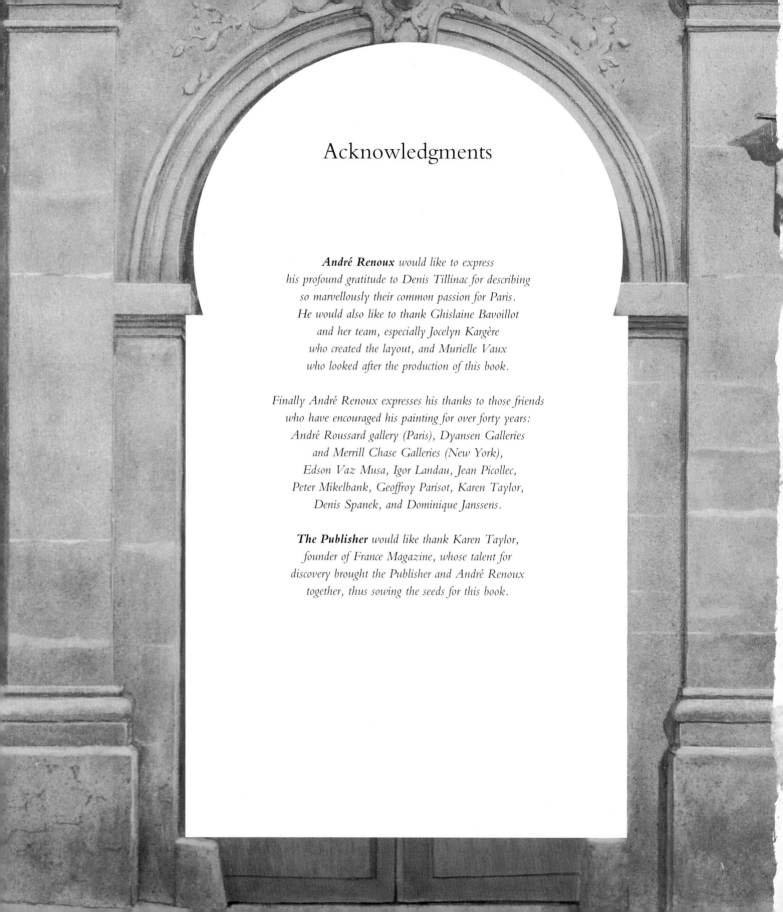

Acknowledgments

*André Renoux would like to express
his profound gratitude to Denis Tillinac for describing
so marvellously their common passion for Paris.
He would also like to thank Ghislaine Bavoillot
and her team, especially Jocelyn Kargère
who created the layout, and Murielle Vaux
who looked after the production of this book.*

*Finally André Renoux expresses his thanks to those friends
who have encouraged his painting for over forty years:
André Roussard gallery (Paris), Dyansen Galleries
and Merrill Chase Galleries (New York),
Edson Vaz Musa, Igor Landau, Jean Picollec,
Peter Mikelbank, Geoffroy Parisot, Karen Taylor,
Denis Spanek, and Dominique Janssens.*

*The Publisher would like thank Karen Taylor,
founder of France Magazine, whose talent for
discovery brought the Publisher and André Renoux
together, thus sowing the seeds for this book.*